Speed Read Anything:
How to Read a Book a Day with Better Retention Than Ever

By Peter Hollins,
Author and Researcher at
petehollins.com

Table of Contents

SPEED READ ANYTHING: *HOW TO READ A BOOK A DAY WITH BETTER RETENTION THAN EVER*   **3**

TABLE OF CONTENTS   **5**

CHAPTER 1. YES, IT'S REAL.   **7**
THE NEUROBIOLOGY OF READING   9
SPEED READING MYTHS   12
SPEED READING BENEFITS   18

CHAPTER 2. PRE-READING IS THE WAY   **25**
THE KBG METHOD   28
THE 4 PS METHOD   34
THE THIEVES FRAMEWORK   40
MAIN IDEAS AND PIVOTAL WORDS   42
MORTIMER ADLER'S 4 LEVELS   46
TRY THE SQ3R   56

CHAPTER 3. SPEED-READING MEAT AND BONES   **75**
STOP SUBVOCALIZATIONS   78
TRAIN YOUR EYES   84
WORD-CHUNKING   92
STRATEGICALLY SKIM   94
MISCELLANEOUS STRATEGIES TO READ FASTER   101

CHAPTER 4. IMPROVING COMPREHENSION AND RETENTION — 107

BASIC TIPS TO IMPROVE COMPREHENSION AND RETENTION — 110
VISUALIZATION — 113
OCULAR FITNESS — 117
READING FOR IDEAS — 122
RETENTION — 124

SUMMARY GUIDE — 133

Chapter 1. Yes, it's real.

If you can read these words, chances are that you know a thing or two about reading. Having said that, there is more to reading than just seeing words, connecting what they mean together, and interpreting the meaning of sentences. Even though most of us can perform this basic function called reading, we are notoriously inefficient at it. We struggle to finish books because we lose focus and give up halfway through, or we simply don't bother reading more than we absolutely have to.

This is a mistake no matter who you are, because reading is arguably the one activity that can single-handedly make you smarter than you are today. It doesn't just add to your knowledge; research shows that it literally alters the composition of your brain through a process called neuroplasticity. Many of the most successful people in the world, such as Bill Gates, Mark Cuban, Elon Musk, and Warren Buffet, are voracious readers and credit their success in part to the knowledge they have gathered from all the books they have read.

If being smarter and more successful weren't enough, reading also makes you a better person by improving your sense of empathy because you're exposed to a multiplicity of different personalities, beliefs, and mindsets. It also reduces stress, and potentially lengthens your lifespan too.

You can enjoy all of these benefits through the simple habit of reading. Though enhancing your knowledge and becoming smarter or more successful is probably the biggest motivator for anyone to read, the important question is this: How exactly do you start reading in order to achieve this goal? In this day and age, few of us have the time to sit down and read books that are hundreds of pages long. Even college students struggle with this, let alone adults with full-time jobs. So, how does one read efficiently?

The answer is to engage in something called speed-reading. Contrary to what the phrase suggests, this doesn't mean you should just cultivate the habit of reading sentences at an extremely high speed. There's much more to it, and we'll explore the concept of speed reading in depth throughout the rest of this book. For now, we'll start by looking at what reading really is from a biological perspective.

The Neurobiology of Reading

As we've briefly discussed, the basic process of reading involves you first detecting words through your eyes, and then mentally interpreting them in the sequence that they appear. Imagine a child who is reading a book for the first time. He sees the words on paper and scans each letter as they appear in individual words and sentences. This part of the process mainly involves your optic nerve and other related bundles.

Once the child's eyes detect the words, he gives some thought to what the words mean together. Here, the middle and back portions of his brain are at work. Two areas in particular are relevant here. These are Broca's area and Wernicke's area. We'll explore these in greater detail.

Broca's Area

The Broca's area lies in the frontal lobe of the brain hemisphere that is dominant in speech production (usually the left). This part of the brain is mainly linked with speech and language processing. So, if you have a certain thought and want to express it out loud, the Broca's area will help you do that. The significance of this area is that it shows how important subvocalization—i.e., mentally vocalizing what we read—can be when absorbing sentences. Damage to the Broca's area prevents people from using grammatically correct speech, and this was found to also impact their ability to understand things that they read. However, as we'll see later, subvocalizations prevent us from speed reading and need to be avoided as far as possible. They served an important purpose when we were children and were first learning to read and comprehend basic language. However, they've now outlived their usefulness.

Wernicke's Area

The Wernicke's area is the second part of the cerebral cortex which is linked to speech and language. However, while the Broca's area is responsible primarily for producing language when we speak, the Wernicke's area is involved in comprehending written and spoken language. Damage to this area of the brain will render a person able to speak fluently, but the sentences will be gibberish because the person has lost the ability to understand the meaning of words.

These two areas are important because when we subvocalize, or repeat words in our head while reading, we perform an extra step of having the Broca's area vocalize what we read. Instead of doing this, you can simply use the Wernicke's area to comprehend your text and move on, thus reducing the time taken to process the sentence and increasing your overall reading speed.

Speed Reading Myths

Before we proceed any further and explore what speed reading really entails, it's important to dispel some commonplace myths about the activity itself. This will help us keep expectations realistic and clarify what the method is really all about.

Myth 1: Speed Reading Is a Myth

The first myth we're going to tackle claims that speed reading in itself is impossible and that you simply can't increase your reading speed significantly without compromising your comprehension of the material you're reading. The fault for this myth becoming popular majorly lies with so-called speed-reading experts themselves. Some of them have claimed that comprehension really doesn't matter while reading, and that sometimes you can simply glance at a page and understand the essence of what's written on it.

However, this is obviously not true. Comprehension is extremely important while reading because if you don't understand the material, then the entire activity becomes useless. You can increase the speed at which you read up to a point before you inevitably start to compromise on comprehension.

Some experts claim that you can read as many as 20,000 or 25,000 words per minute and still understand everything. Yet this isn't true. It is biologically impossible for us to read that fast because our eyes simply cannot scan words at such a high speed. As we've discussed, when you read, you fix your eyes on a certain sentence, take in all the words you see, and formulate the meaning of all the words stitched together before moving on to the next sentence. There is a limit to how fast your eyes can conduct this process.

Some experts have tried to weasel out of this limitation by simply taking in more information at a time. So instead of reading one sentence at a time, you read entire paragraphs before moving on. The problem with this is that again, our eyes are limited in the ways that they can absorb words. They can only take in so many words before needing to move to take in more.

Our eyes are not the only aspect of our biology to blame. It's difficult for our brain to process information from multiple lines simultaneously because we have limited working memory. What ends up happening is that we don't absorb all the information we have taken in, resulting in weaker comprehension. So, to what extent can we increase our reading speed? This brings us to the next speed-reading myth.

Myth 2: Even Moderate Gains in Reading Speed Result in Weak Comprehension

This myth needs to be treated somewhat carefully because this can be true in certain circumstances, but it is not *necessarily* true if you apply speed-reading techniques in ways that prioritize comprehension. You can definitely increase your reading speed without losing comprehension, but if you're solely focused on reading as quickly as possible, you will end up compromising on quality.

The science on how fast you can read while still understanding everything is about 500-600 words per minute. This appears to be a hard limit, and anything above 600 words per minute will result in you losing out on understanding. The average college-educated reader has a speed of about 300 wpm, which means that it is theoretically possible for you to double your reading speed.

However, if you see claims about people reading any faster than that, they are likely skipping paragraphs and pages in order to claim that they can go through books quickly. Some books, such as those in the non-fiction genre, do allow you to do that without losing the essence of what's being said, but if you're reading heavier material, you might need to reduce your speed and re-read sentences multiple times to fully understand them. It all depends on how and where you apply your speed-reading skills.

One important thing to note here is that it can be easy to fall into the trap of simply reading as fast as possible and assuring yourself that you've understood everything when you really haven't. Speed-reading can be a boon when used correctly, but when applied indiscriminately, you will lose out on comprehension and cultivate unhealthy reading habits which do not prioritize learning.

Myth 3: Speed-Reading Techniques Do Not Work

According to proponents of this myth, you can become a faster reader, but speed-reading techniques are not going to help you with that. Instead, you simply need to read more often to get used to processing information at a faster speed. You need not do anything special besides actually reading, because your reading speed will grow organically.

As with the first myth, part of the blame for this myth lies with speed-reading experts themselves for making outlandish claims. In this case, the claim is that subvocalization should be avoided at all times while speed reading because it slows your words per minute rate down. Subvocalization is simply an inner voice you have which reads words aloud in your head. As a child, you might have spoken your words out loud because they helped you understand them better. This is the same process, only it happens entirely in your head, and it is equally important where comprehension is concerned.

The problem with this claim is that it appears to state a universal truth. The fact of the matter is that in some cases, such as when you're reading complex material or simply reading for pleasure, subvocalizations can be desirable cause they aid either understanding or enjoyment of the text. However, in other scenarios, subvocalizations can effectively be curbed in order to increase your reading speed.

If you want to test whether speed-reading techniques actually work right now, here's a trick for you. Use a pointer (a pen, pencil, or even your finger) as you read and keep underlining text. The utility of this technique is that it reduces the rate at which your eyes wander by keeping them fixed at certain points. When it works for you, you'll know speed-reading is real.

Speed Reading Benefits

In the previous section we covered some things that aren't true of speed reading, and here we'll explore some things that *are* true about speed-reading techniques. These are the various benefits you can derive from practicing speed reading. Though all of these will take some time to develop, you'll notice them sooner rather than later.

Benefit 1: Improved Memory

At first glance, memory might not seem like it has much to do with reading. But this couldn't be further from the truth. When we read, our brains continuously make use of our working memory to retain the words we take in and interpret them accurately. Once we've figured out what the various sentences mean, the brain also stores the information for later use. Reading enhances your ability to retain large amounts of information, and speed reading pushes your brain to do even better because of the speed at which you need to process words.

Benefit 2: Better Focus

This is a much more intuitively obvious benefit since speed reading demands that your entire focus is dedicated to reading. This is the only way you can read fast, and letting your mind wander would defeat the entire purpose of using speed-reading techniques. As you practice speed reading, your mind will become adept at staying focused on reading, which will become an invaluable skill for other areas of your life.

Benefit 3: Higher Levels of Confidence

Too many people are intimidated by books, especially long, verbose ones. However, once you master speed-reading techniques, you'll be able to work through and comprehend even the most challenging books with relative ease. You'll also be able to do so at a much quicker pace than most others. It's easy to see how this skill might breed confidence. You'll have the assurance of knowing that no matter what book, article, newspaper, etc., is put in front of you, you can understand it well and expand your knowledge base in ways that most others struggle to do.

Benefit 4: Improved Logic

When you speed read, your brain is processing tons of information in a short span of time. This can often make it easier to spot logical flaws and things that don't make sense in the material you're reading.

With practice, your brain improves significantly at sorting information, finding correlations and connections with other bits of knowledge you've consumed recently, and developing your own unique analysis of the material at hand. This improvement in logic takes place alongside the gains in memory, and both work in tandem to help you see your reading material in a new light.

Takeaways

- Reading in the way we normally do can take far too long. In the present day and age, we often don't have the time to sit through hundreds of pages of books. To solve this issue, we must learn how to read faster so that we can get on with our lives. That's what speed reading is all about.
- Speed reading primarily involves two areas of your brain, the Broca's area and Wernicke's area. While the former is involved in language production, the latter controls language comprehension. As we'll see later, these areas are very

important when it comes to reducing subvocalizations, which will involve skipping the function of the Broca's area and relying solely on the Wernicke's area.
- Several myths about speed reading abound on the internet. The biggest of these is that speed reading is a myth and does not help you read faster. This is decidedly false. Another common myth is that one can train themselves to read tens of thousands of words per minute, which is not humanly possible. A third myth is that subvocalizations are essential to understanding words properly. While this may be true in some cases, it is certainly not accurate in all of them.
- There are many benefits of speed reading that you can come to experience as you practice the techniques in this book. These include improvements in logic since you engage with texts better, gains in memory and focus because you can only read faster when you concentrate on your text fully, and higher confidence from all the

knowledge you'll have acquired in a short period of time.

Chapter 2. Pre-Reading is the Way

The phrase "speed reading" gives the impression that you simply need to train yourself to go through words and sentences at a quicker pace to get through books faster. While that is definitely an important part of speed reading, it doesn't encapsulate the entire picture. Another essential part of speed reading is something called pre-reading. When you pre-read a book, you're preparing yourself and gathering as much relevant information as you can before you actually start reading the book. The process of pre-reading is unique for every book, but there are some basic strategies that you can uniformly apply to help you pre-read successfully.

At this stage, you might be wondering, why do we need to pre-read at all? Why not just get started as soon as possible? Pre-reading is important because most of us pick up a particular book with a certain intention. We're either looking to learn something new or explore some specific theme the book delves into. Pre-reading will help you get the most out of the books you read without having to go through them from cover to cover. With certain books, especially non-fiction ones, we often don't start out with all the requisite knowledge we need to understand the book properly. This means that when we read, we end up spending much more time trying to figure out what's being said, its relevance, etc., than we would if we had the information we needed to begin with.

Pre-reading also acquaints you with what topics exactly the book in question covers, the gist of the author's arguments, and how much time and attention you'll need to read the relevant parts of the book. You can gather this information by simply going through certain parts of the book, such as the preface, introduction, chapter summaries, and various headings within the chapters. This is but one of the many things you can do to successfully pre-read, and in this chapter, we'll discuss some of the most effective tips and tricks you can use.

Previewing a Text

Previewing a text is probably the simplest form of pre-reading it. On the most basic level, it only entails familiarizing yourself with what the book is about. So for example, its fairly clear from a title such as *Freakonomics: A Rogue Economist Explores the Rogue Side of Everything* that this book is related to economics. If the title does not make it immediately obvious, reading the synopsis or index of the text will likely do the job. While this is one simple way to preview a text, there are also more extensive ways to get to know your text better, as discussed below.

The KBG Method

The KBG method of previewing texts attempts to clarify your knowledge, biases, and goals with respect to a certain text. There are three main steps to be followed in this method.

Step One

First, you need do something very similar to the basic previewing strategy we outlined earlier. Get to know the overarching theme or topic of the book by either reading the title, synopsis, or index, whichever shines the most light on this question. Next, you'll want to flip through the pages and get a general idea of what the bold-faced headings across the book relate to.

Some texts tend to have a heading every few pages, which makes it unfeasible to go through all of them in the interest of time. But at the very least, ensure that you've perused through enough headings in each chapter to understand the gist of the discussion in those parts of the book.

Finally, you'll want to have a look at any and all graphic aids, as well as the accompanying captions littered across the book. This serves the same purpose as flipping through the headings.

Step Two

For the *second* part of this method, we'll go a little deeper and build upon the knowledge we've acquired through our preliminary preview of the text. By reading the title and subheadings, we've acquired a superficial idea of what the book is about. Now, we're going to try and grasp how the book discusses the main themes relevant to it.

The first step here is to read the introduction. Depending on what kind of book you're reading, the introduction usually does a great job of summarizing all the various themes, ideas, and arguments a book explores in the space of 10-20 pages. As such, this is the most important part of the second step because the introduction is likely to give you the most useful information that you'll need. If you're short on time, it might be advisable to do this and skip the other parts of this step.

Once you're done with the introduction, if you have additional time, you'll want to move on to the subheadings again. However, this time, you should read the first line after every heading. The first line usually reveals enough about the subheadings to give you a decent idea of what's going to be discussed in that section.

Next, you're going to want to read the conclusion at the end of the book. The conclusion will summarize all the main themes and arguments the book has covered in a succinct manner, so when you actually sit down to read the book it will all seem much more familiar to you. Lastly, if your text has a list of study questions or topics listed at the end of each chapter, you can go through those as well. These are inevitably going to be connected to the main content of that particular chapter and will further enhance your familiarity with its material.

Step Three

This wraps up the second step and now we finally get to the KBG part of the KBG method. As mentioned earlier, K stands for (prior) knowledge, B for biases, and G for goals, and this final step will involve you exploring these in relation to the text you're about to read. A good way to go about this step is to draw a rough table with three columns. The first column merely states what each initial stands for. The second column contains a question that relates to each of these three aspects. So, the first row in this column should have the question, "What do I already know about the subject of this text?" The second row should contain, "What are my biases on this topic?"

Finally, the third row should ask, "What do I want to learn as I read this text?" The third column must contain the answers to these questions. Keep referencing this table as you read to remind yourself of the reason you picked up this text and to maximize your learning from it.

Let's look at this step with the help of an example, using the book *Freakonomics* like we did earlier. From the earlier preview, you now know that the book is related to economics, and after going through the first two steps of the KBG method you've familiarized yourself with the content of the book. Now, you need to answer the three questions in the table.

The first question is, "What do I already know about the subject of this text?" Maybe you're familiar with the law of supply and demand wherein demand for a good increases when supply decreases and vice versa. Maybe you also know about the concept of utility in economics, which is the units of satisfaction a person derives from the consumption of a particular good, and related concepts like diminishing marginal utility. Note all of these down in the box. If they come up in the text, you can spend less time on these topics because you're already familiar with them, and reading about them all over again will probably only result in minimal benefit.

Now you need to consider your biases in relation to economics or "pop economics," as books like *Freakonomics* are known for. It's possible that you believe such books try to present superficial analysis as something in-depth or that they bend facts in order to make content appear more interesting than it really is. Or you might think that looking at issues from an economic perspective is only one of many ways to analyze something, and that on its own it probably isn't reflective of the truth. All of these are potential biases that will reduce how much you can learn from a book like *Freakonomics*, and it will help to be cognizant of these beliefs as you read the book.

Lastly, you need to assess your goals or desired learning outcomes from this text. You could be wanting to learn more about economic principles in a way that is fun, approachable, and yet contains enough depth to help you in your ordinary or academic life. Alternatively, you might be curious about how one can analyze issues from an economic, as opposed to a psychological, sociological, or political, perspective. Perhaps you've never properly used statistics and economic principles or concepts to look at things like why parents are late to pick up their kids from daycare.

In sum, the KBG method is an excellent way for you to maximize how much you learn from a given text, since it forces you to lay out things you already know, biases that block knowledge, and what your specific goals are regarding the book so you can focus exclusively on them as you peruse your text. Moreover, going through the introduction, subheadings, conclusion, etc., will also familiarize you with the contents of the book, which will make things seem much less complex when you read through the text. This will greatly increase your reading speed, while also ensuring that you learn as much as possible.

The 4 Ps Method

As you'll see in this chapter, the KBG method is only one of three great ways to preview a text. The method that we'll discuss in this section is called the 4 Ps method. As you might have guessed already, *previewing* is one of the four Ps, along with *purpose*, *prior knowledge*, and *predict*. Let's go through what each of these involves one by one.

The first of the four Ps is purpose. This refers to the reasons why you're reading the particular text you've chosen and what you aim to get out of it. Your purpose will have an impact on the kind of reading strategies you employ and how carefully you read the text. For example, if you're reading a fiction book, you can afford to read faster and with somewhat lower concentration since there isn't as much technical information as in non-fiction.

While trying to determine your purpose, there are a few questions you can ask to help yourself. Ask yourself whether you're looking for discussion on general ideas and themes such as poverty in a Dickens novel, or for specific details on, say, economics from a book like *Freakonomics*. Another question to ask yourself is whether you'll be using the text for an assignment in class, if it's going to be discussed with someone else like a reading group, or is it a part of the syllabus for an exam? This will help you read the text in a more appropriate manner so that you can fulfill your purpose more easily.

Lastly, ask yourself how this text fits into the larger scheme of your goals and concerns. If you're trying to familiarize yourself with economics, how is *Freakonomics* helping you do that? How is it *not* helping you? Questions like these sharpen your focus on the most important bits that you want to glean from the book, making reading the text easier and faster.

The second P is preview. We've discussed this in fair detail already, but some of the essentials you'll want to go through are the title, first and last paragraphs of the text (for shorter pieces), all the various headings and subheadings, and the introduction. All of this should be more than enough to give you a fair idea about what the text discusses, its main arguments and themes, etc.

The third P in this method is prior knowledge. Just as we did when discussing the K in the KBG method, assessing prior knowledge simply entails trying to ascertain what you already know about the main topic of your text. If you're reading *Sapiens* by Yuval Noah Harari, ask yourself how much you know about history, especially ancient history. Once you're sure of what you already know, you can spend less time on those aspects and concentrate more on everything you still wish to learn instead.

The last of the four Ps is predict. When you finish with the first three Ps, try to predict as accurately as you can what the writer is going to say about the various topics and subtopics you've come across. This will heighten your interest in the text, and over time you'll get better at predicting the author's focus. Being able to predict what an author will say accurately is uniquely satisfying, and that adds to the motivation we're seeking to build here.

Let's see how the four Ps method works with the help of an example. Let's use the same one that we utilized for the KBG method—the *Freakonomics* book. The first P is purpose, and we've covered this before briefly. Some goals that you might have are learning more about economics, or about how various incentives figure into our decisions, and how to conduct economic analysis in general.

The second P is previewing. This part is fairly straightforward since you only need to go through the aforementioned parts of the book and get a better idea of all the topics the book covers.

The third P is prior knowledge. Make a list of everything you already know about economics and economic analysis so that you can devote less time to these and focus instead on what you don't know, as well as what forms a part of your learning goals.

Lastly, the fourth P is predicting. By now you probably know that the book focuses on the role of incentives in our lives. From this, one can predict that the author is going to connect incentives with decision-making, and talk about how when we make decisions, we implicitly weigh the pros and cons and try to influence outcomes accordingly. This is one example of the way you can predict things. The more topics a book deals with, the more opportunities you have to predict.

As you can see, the 4 Ps method does incorporate a lot of what we discussed in the KBG method. Two of the major factors that must influence choosing one method over the other are the amount of time you have and the length of the text you're reading. The KBG method is more suitable for longer texts like books, whereas the 4 Ps method is more appropriate for shorter ones like articles, novellas, and the like.

Regarding time, the KBG method clearly takes more time than the 4 Ps method, but it also results in better learning outcomes because your previewing is more thorough in the former. You could use the 4 Ps method for a longer text as well if you're especially short on time, but keep the tradeoff you'll be making in mind.

The THIEVES Framework

The third and final previewing method we will discuss is called the THIEVES method. The initials stand for:

Titles
Headings
Introduction
Every first sentence
Visuals
End of chapter questions
Summary/conclusion

In the previous section, we noted that the 4 Ps method is a shorter version of the KBG method. The THIEVES Method is an even shorter version of both and is meant to be finished in just five minutes. The two things that will take you the most amount of time here are obviously the introduction and summary or conclusion. For this method, you only need to superficially skim through both because the idea is just to familiarize yourself with the broad themes and topics that your text deals with.

Let's see this with the help of, yet again, *Freakonomics*. You start with reading the full title of the book, which is Freakonomics: *A Rogue Economist Explores the Rogue Side of Everything*. Then you proceed to the various headings within the book, though there aren't too many in this one. As such, you can just read the chapter headings. Next comes the introduction, which is about 13 pages long. Skim through it quickly over a minute at the most. After this, read the first sentence of every chapter since the book has very few headings as such.

The book doesn't have too many visuals, so you can skip this part of the method as well as the end of chapter questions. Lastly, the book doesn't have summaries, but the last paragraphs of each chapter do a good job of shedding light on the content of that chapter. Skim through these and you'll be done with the THIEVES method of previewing a text.

Main Ideas and Pivotal Words

As you might've been able to tell from our discussion of previewing, the main purpose here is to become familiar with the overarching themes and ideas discussed in the book. We covered three frameworks that will help you achieve this goal with any text you read. In this section, we'll go over some more tips you can utilize not only while previewing texts, but also while reading them in general.

The first major topic of discussion for this section is skimming for main ideas. As you go through the various sections of the text highlighted above, such as the headings, introduction and conclusion, the first lines of every heading, etc., there are certain keywords you should look out for. These include *causes, effects, results, versus,* and *pros and cons*, among others.

The reason these words are important is that they generally flag the most essential parts of a text's content. The first three words are all indicative of some correlative or causative connection being drawn between two or more things, whereas the latter two highlight a contrast between different sets of arguments or factors that influence a particular outcome or event. As you keep a lookout for these words more often, your eyes will automatically become more accustomed to spotting them in texts, and you'll be able to jump to the relevant parts quicker than before.

A related concept is that of pivotal words. Once you train yourself to recognize them, you'll easily be able to tell what the author is going to say next, and so you can process faster and increase your overall reading speed. There are many different types of pivotal words, and they're listed below.

Additive words: Also, further, moreover, and, furthermore, too, besides, in addition. These tend to indicate that something closely related to what has already been said is going to be mentioned.

Equivalent words: As well as, at the same time, similarly, equally important, likewise. These indicate that a comparison is going to be drawn between two similar things

Amplification words: For example (e.g.), specifically, as, for instance, such as, like. These are used to expand upon what's been said through the use of examples.

Alternative words: Either/or, other than, neither/nor, otherwise. These draw a dichotomy between two disparate things.

Repetitive words: Again, in other words, to repeat, that is (i.e.). These repeat what's been said for emphasis.

Contrast and change words: But, on the contrary, still, conversely, on the other hand, though, despite, instead of, yet, however, rather than, regardless, nevertheless, even though, whereas, in spite of, notwithstanding. Similar to alternative words.

Cause and effect words: Accordingly, since, then, because, so, thus, consequently, hence, therefore, for this reason. These denote correlation or causation between elements.

Qualifying words: If, although, unless, providing, whenever. These add a condition or qualifier to what has been said.

Concession words: Accepting the data, granted that, of course. These express agreement with something that was mentioned.

Emphasizing words: Above all, more important, indeed. These are meant to draw your attention to something.

Order words: Finally, second, then, first, next, last. These are meant to add structure to the writing.

Time words: Afterwards, meanwhile, now, before, subsequently, presently, formerly, ultimately, previously, later. Similar to order words, these flag the flow of a text.

Summarizing words: For these reasons, in brief, in conclusion, to sum up. These summarize what's been said.

Though this might seem like a long list, you'll eventually get used to it if you make a conscious effort to spot these pivotal words while reading in the future. It might help to have a list of these handy when you do sit down to read, because in the long run being able to spot these words will greatly enhance your reading speed.

Mortimer Adler's 4 Levels

How do you take in the information you need and really read to effectively increase your knowledge?

Enter: the *four levels of reading,* and it was developed by philosopher Mortimer Adler in his suitably titled publication *How to Read a Book.* Adler explains that reading is not a single, universally consistent act. He breaks up the act of reading into four individual levels that differ in purpose, effort, and the amount of time they take. Furthermore, different tiers apply to different kinds of reading—some books can be appropriate for all levels, while others just support one or two. Especially in the higher two levels, faithfully following these tiers of reading will greatly advance your expertise on the subject.

Adler's four levels of reading, from simplest to most complex, are:

- Elementary
- Inspectional
- Analytical
- Syntopical

Elementary. You're already past this level. This is, essentially, learning to read. It's the kind of reading that's taught in elementary school. You're learning what the letters are, how words are pronounced, and what they objectively mean. It's knowing that the sentence "The cat is on the bed" means there's a cat on the bed, and that it *doesn't* say there's a dog on the couch. Blows the mind, right?

The elementary stage also applies to an adult who's learning a new language and has to be trained to understand new alphabets, vocabulary, and pronunciation. It also describes a student reading a technical textbook for the first time who has to learn new syntax or specific jargon. Anytime you come upon a new language, dialect, or lexicon, you're doing elementary reading.

Inspectional. The next level up for readers is understanding the essence of a certain book—but not digesting the whole of it. It's called the inspectional stage, and it's sometimes disparaged or discounted by avid readers. But in developing expertise, it's a very valuable process.

Inspectional reading actually has two mini-stages of its own:

- *Systematic skimming.* This is casually examining certain elements of a book apart from the body of the text: skimming the table of contents and the index, or reading the preface or the blurb on the back inside jacket. If you're assessing an e-book, it could mean reading the online description and customer reviews as well. Systematic skimming gives you enough information to know what the book is and how you would classify it: "it's a novel about World War II," or "it's a book that explains how to cook French cuisine." That's it.

- *Superficial reading.* This stage is actually reading the book but in a very casual way. You start at the beginning and take in the material without consuming it or thinking too much about it. You don't make notes in the margins. You don't look up unfamiliar phrases or concepts—if there's a passage you don't understand, you just proceed to the next part. In superficial reading, you're getting a sense of the tone, rhythm, and general direction of the book, rather than absorbing every single element of the narrative.

Inspectional reading is something like a recon mission or a survey. You're just getting a sense of what the book is about and the reading experience. You might pick up on a couple of very broad, general ideas in the book, but you won't go very deeply into them. You'll just find out what you might be in for, and then you'll decide whether you're interested enough to go more in-depth.

For example, let's say you're looking at a book on classical music. In your systematic skimming, you'd see the title and subtitle. You'd read the back flap, which says it's "an in-depth but gently irreverent study of classical composers." You'd read the table of contents—there are chapters entitled "Wagner in Drag," "Mozart's Cat Imitations," and "Beethoven's Love of Rats." At this point, you've probably ascertained that this is *not* a terribly serious work and not one that's likely to add to your expertise, although it may be entertaining.

Why should a budding expert go through this stage and not just skip to the next level? Even though it's not a deep dive, it gives you a lot of answers. You'll get a sense of the writer's approach: is it serious, comical, or satirical? Does it rely on real-life accounts or imaginary situations? Is it heavy on statistics? Does it quote a lot of outside sources? Are there pictures?

Having a good sense of the answers to those questions will help you frame the content and define your expectations, which—if you've decided to proceed with the book—will make the next level of reading more productive.

Analytical. The third level of reading is the deepest level for consuming a single book or volume of work—it's full digestion of, *and interaction with*, the material at hand. The challenge of analytical reading is simply: "If time were not an object, how thoroughly would you read this book?"

Analytical reading can be described as taking the book out of the author's hands and making it your own. You don't just read the text; you highlight or underline key points, and you make commentary or ask questions. In a way, you can use the marginalia to simulate an ongoing conversation with the writer.

The goal of analytical reading is to understand the material well enough so you can explain it to someone else without a lot of effort. You're able to describe the subject very concisely. You're able to list its parts in order and say how they connect with each other. You're able to understand and specify the issues the writer's concerned with and what problems they're trying to resolve.

For example, if you're reading Stephen Hawking's *A Brief History of Time*, you'd highlight key phrases in the first part about the history of physics: the Big Bang theory, black holes, and time travel, for example. You might asterisk the names of Copernicus and Galileo with a note to research them more fully. You might question Hawking's explanation of the expanding universe with writing in the margins.

Analytical reading is hard work. But it's the level at which the thrill of gaining new understanding is most profound and rewarding. This kind of interaction with reading makes learning proactive—instead of just listening to what some person's telling you, it's more like you're extracting the information yourself. When you're doing that, you're engaging more of your mind, and that means it's far more likely you're going to *remember* what you've learned. That's a much easier path toward expertise.

Syntopical. In the final level of reading, you work with multiple books or pieces of material covering the same subject. One could describe syntopical reading as "compare/contrast," but it's actually a lot deeper than that. (And syntopical reading is not to be confused with the similarly spelled *synoptical* reading, which is pretty much its exact opposite.)

At this stage, you're trying to understand the entire breadth of the subject you're studying, not just a single volume about it. Sound familiar? You analyze the differences in the ideas, syntax, and arguments presented in the books and compare them. You're able to identify and fill any gaps in knowledge you might have. You're conversing with multiple partners, forming and arranging the most pressing questions you need to answer. You're identifying all the issues and aspects of the subjects that the books cover and looking up phraseology and vocabulary that you don't understand.

Syntopical reading is a relatively major commitment, almost like a semester-long college course you're teaching yourself. Think of it as an active effort, something one doesn't normally associate with the relaxing act of reading a novel.

It's like a TV show or movie in which someone's trying to unravel a multilayered criminal enterprise. Somewhere in the movie, they show a giant bulletin board in the station with drawings, Post-its, and pictures of people, with pieces of yarn showing how they're all interconnected. When new information is discovered from different sources, it all gets added to that board. That's what syntopical reading is like: it's a concerted effort to find the answers and increase your expertise, and you don't even have to deal with the mob. You can concentrate on more lawful subjects like Occam's razor, absurdist theater, or the stock market.

These four levels serve as connected steps that gradually make a subject approachable, more relevant, and finally, fully familiar to you.

In the elementary stage—well, you're learning to read. You kind of need that for everything.

In the inspectional phase, you're getting an overview of the framework and structure and gauging your interest. You're priming yourself in case you decide to commit to the analytical phase by estimating what's in store for you at a deeper level.

In the analytical phase, you're committing to an extensive effort to understand as much of the subject as you can from as many viewpoints as possible. You're absorbing and questioning the book, and creating further curiosity about the topic it addresses, driving yourself to learn more.

In the syntopical phase, you've "graduated," in a sense, from a single or limited perspective of the subject to a holistic study of all its elements. This is where you're layering the levels of your expertise at multiple points—something you can't even comprehend in typically casual or recreational reading.

Try the SQ3R

This final method of pre-reading is all about how to interact with a set of information before and after.

The technique is called The SQ3R method, named for its five components:

- survey
- question
- read
- recite
- review

Survey. The first step in the method is getting a general overview of what you'll be reading. Textbooks and nonfiction works aren't like fiction or narrative literature in which you just start from the beginning and wind your way through each chapter. The best works of nonfiction are arranged to impart information in a way that's clear and memorable and builds upon each previous chapter. If you dive in without surveying first, you are going in blind, without understanding where you're heading and what you're trying to accomplish. You should get a lay of the land first, *before* you delve into Chapter 1. The survey component allows you to get the most general introduction to the topic so you can establish and shape the goals you want to achieve from reading the book.

It's just like taking a look at the entire map before you set off on a road trip. You may not need all the knowledge at the moment, but understanding everything as a whole and how it fits together will help you with the small details and when you're in the weeds. You'll know that you generally need to head southwest if you're confused.

In the SQ3R method, surveying means examining the structure of the work: the book title, the introduction or preface, section titles, chapter titles, headings and subheadings. If the book is illustrated with pictures or graphics, you'd review them. You could also make note of the conventions the book uses to guide your reading: typefaces, bold or italic text, and chapter objectives and study questions if they're in there. In using the survey step, you're setting up expectations for what you're going to be reading about and giving yourself an initial framework to structure your goals for reading the material.

For example, let's say you're reading a book to learn more about geology. I happen to have one called *Geology Illustrated* by John S. Shelton—it's about fifty years old and no longer in print, but it works fine for our purposes.

There's a preface describing what's in the book and how the illustrations are arranged. There's an unusually extensive table of contents, divided into parts: "Materials," "Structure," "Sculpture," "Time," "Case Histories," and "Implications." That tells me that the book will start with concrete (excuse the pun) geological elements, will flow into how they form over time, important incidents, and what we might expect in the future. That's a pretty good guess at the arc of the book.

Each part is then divided into chapters, which are further divided into a ton of headings and subheadings—too many to mention here, but they give a more nuanced summary of what each part will go into. When you survey and know the significance of what you're currently learning, you are able to instantly comprehend it better. It's the difference between looking at a single gear in isolation versus seeing where and how it works in a complex clock.

Beyond books, you should survey all the important concepts in a discipline. If you can't find it within a structure like a book's table of contents, then you need to be able to create it for yourself. Yes, this is the difficult part, but once you are able to lay all the concepts out and understand how they relate to each other at least on a surface level, you will already be leaps ahead of others. Use the survey component to form an outline of what you'll learn. In a sense, it's more like you're plotting out a metaphorical "book" for yourself.

You want to form a general outline of what you're going to learn. Since you're studying this on your own, there might be a few gaps in what you think you'll need to know. So in this phase, you'll determine exactly what you *want* to become knowledgeable about, as specifically as you can. For example, if you want to learn all about psychology, that's going to take a significant amount of time. It won't happen in one shot. You'd want to specify it a little more: the early history of psychoanalysis, the works of Sigmund Freud and Carl Jung, sports psychology, developmental psychology—the possibilities are plenty.

You'll want to keep an eye out for phrases or concepts that appear in several different sources, since they represent elements that come up often in your chosen field and might be things you have to know. Draw connections and cause-and-effect relationships before even diving into any of the concepts in detail.

For example, let's say you want to study the history of European cinema. Entering "European cinema history" into Google brings up a lot of interesting possibilities, and some of those can be used to form the outline you want.

You can look for reading materials on Amazon.com, finding the ones that seem the most authoritative. The Internet Movie Database (IMDB) can help you find the most important European films for you to watch. You can discover which European directors are the most cited and appear to be the most important and influential. You can research which European movies are the highest rated and why. You can collect a few resources on what specific countries had what cinematic movements and why.

Then you'll organize these resources. You'll come up with a plan to study each one—perhaps study a chapter in a book on early European film history, then watch a couple of films that represent the era you're on at the moment and give yourself a film review assignment afterward. Focus on gathering and organizing; you don't need to touch these resources yet. The important aspect is that you've surveyed the topic before diving in and thus understand what you're getting into and why.

Question. In the second stage of the SQ3R method, you're still not diving into the deep end. During the question stage, you'll work a little more deeply to get your mind more prepared to focus and interact with the material you're reading. You'll take a slightly closer look at the structure of the book and form some questions you'd like to answer or set up the objectives you want to achieve.

In the question phase of reading a book—or, more precisely at this point, *preparing* to read—you'd go through the chapter titles, headings, and subheadings and rephrase them in the form of a question. This turns the dry title the author has given into a challenge or problem for you to solve. For example, if you're reading a book on Freud, there might be a chapter called "Foundations of Freud's Analyses of Dreams." You'd rewrite this chapter title as "How did Sigmund Freud's work on dream interpretation originate and what were his very first ideas on the subject?" You could pencil that question in the margin of your book. If you're reading a textbook with study questions at the ends of the chapters, those serve as excellent guides to what you're about to find out.

In the geology book, I'm afraid there aren't too many chapter titles that I could rephrase as inquiries. ("Weathering," "Groundwater," "Glaciation"—that's about it.) But there are headings that might work: "Some Effects of Metamorphism on Sedimentary Rocks," for example, can become "What can happen to bottom-centered rocks through eons of environmental change?" Not only have I changed it to a question, but I've paraphrased the title into wording that I can understand even before I've started reading.

Now that you've organized your resources for study planning, you can arrange some of the topics you're going to cover into questions you want answered or objectives that you want to meet. Based on the source material you've lined up and the patterns that you might have observed, what specific answers are you hoping to find in your studies? Write them down. This is also a good time to come up with a structure for answering your questions—a daily journal, a self-administered quiz, some kind of "knowledge tracker"? You don't have to answer the questions yet—you just need to know how you're going to record them when you do.

In our European film history example, if you've done even the most cursory investigation in the survey phase, you undoubtedly came across some directors' names more than once: Federico Fellini, Jean-Luc Godard, Luis Buñuel, Fritz Lang, and so forth. You figure they're going to be important people to get to know, so you could ask the question, "Why was Fellini so influential?" "What was Buñuel's directing style?" "What themes did Godard pursue in his filmmaking?" You might have come across certain concepts or themes that seemed common in European film—"French New Wave," "World War II," "neo-realism," for example. Put these down as targets for your study and arrange them into your outline.

Reading. In this stage you're finally ready to dive into the material. Because you've gotten the lay of the land and formed some questions and goals for your studies, you're a little more engaged when you finally sit down to read. You're looking for answers to the questions you've raised. Another underrated aspect of formulating and organizing before you actually begin reading is to build *anticipation* for learning. You've been looking over everything for a while now, and you'll probably be eager to finally dive in and answer the questions you've been mentally accumulating.

This step is where most people try to start but fail because they lack a foundation and instead have unreasonable expectations.

Now you're being deliberate and paced about your reading so you can comprehend better. This means slowing down—a *lot.* Be patient with the material and with yourself. If a passage is difficult to understand, read it extremely slowly. If you aren't getting a sense of clarity about a certain part, stop, go back to the beginning, and reread it. It's not like you're reading a page-turner novel that you can't put down. You're taking in information that might be densely packed—so read it slowly and attentively, one section at a time.

Chances are that reading is part of your study plan, but so might be visual aids, online courses, and Internet resources. Use them exactly the way you'd use the book in the reading phase: deliberately and persistently, with the goal of fully understanding each concept you're being taught. If you get lost, remember the rewind button and scrolling are your best buddies. Plan your study time around getting as complete a level of comprehensiveness as you can.

With our European film history example, this is obvious. Watch your films with a critical eye. At certain points you might want to rewind to catch visual images, dialogue, or action that might be pertinent. If you can watch a video with a director's commentary audio track, you'll want to spend an afternoon with that. Cross-check the movies with the books you're reading or the online courses you're taking to answer any questions or lines of thought that you might have.

Reciting. This step is crucial in processing the information you're learning and is the biggest difference between reading to learn and reading for entertainment. Now that you're familiar with the material, the aim of the reciting phase is to reorient your mind and attention to focus and learn more fully as you go along. In other words, this step is about literal recitation.

Ask questions—out loud, verbally—about what you're reading. This is also the point where you take copious notes in the margins of the text and underline or highlight key points. Recitation is verbal and also through writing. However, it's important to restate these points *in your own words* rather than just copy phrases from the book onto a piece of paper. By doing this, you're taking the new knowledge and putting it into phrases of which you already know the meaning. This makes the information easier to grasp in a language you understand. It makes it significant and meaningful to you.

My geology book happens to have pretty wide margins on the sides of the pages, so I have some nice room to rephrase and rewrite key points as well as highlight important concepts. For example, consider the following original text:

> "This comparison suggests that the slow progress of erosion on hills and mountains is similar to the much more rapid and observable changes seen in miniature all about us."

I could rewrite the above into something like this:

> "Mountains and hills experience the same decay as happens in lowlands and rivers, just more slowly. Similar to baseball players."

What I'm doing here is putting one single bit of information into two distinct phrases, one of which I had to come up with myself. This is a huge tool that's used in memorization, and it's also a great way to make the information more meaningful to me personally. I also added a bit about baseball because I like baseball, and it makes the concept instantly understandable when I look back at it. Repeated throughout the course of a whole book, this process multiplies your learning capacity by itself.

The recitation phase in organizing your studies is great because it works across different mediums, and there are plenty of ways you can express your questions and restatements.

Going back to our European cinema example, if you're watching Ingmar Bergman's *The Seventh Seal* (short summary: medieval knight meets angel of death, tries to buy time by playing chess with him), you might write down questions about its Biblical references, the art direction, the Middle Ages references, or the cinematography. You could also write a summary or do a video blog of the movie and address the key sequences that are most relevant to your questions. You could also compare it to other films by Bergman or note similarities his style has with other directors that you're studying. The important part is that you are taking the time to rephrase and recite new knowledge and make it meaningful to you—and no one else.

Review. The final stage of the SQ3R plan is when you go back over the material that you've studied, re-familiarize yourself with the most important points, and build your skills at memorizing the material.

Robinson breaks this stage down into specific days of the week, but we'll just mention some of the tactics in general. They include writing more questions about important parts you have highlighted, orally answering some of the questions if you can, reviewing your notes, creating flashcards for important concepts and terminology, rewriting the table of contents using your own words, and building out a mind map. Any kind of practice that helps you drill down, take in, and commit information to memory is fair game (though flashcards are especially effective).

This step is meant to strengthen your memory of the material, but it does more than that. It can help you see connections and similarities between different aspects that you might not have picked up at first and put concepts and ideas into greater context. It can also improve your mental organization skills so you can use this practice for other topics.

Think of this step as the natural continuation of the survey step. At this point, you've gained an outline of the field, you've gotten into the nitty-gritty, and now you should take a step back, reevaluate, and make updated, more accurate, and insightful connections. Pair that with memorization, and your path to self-learning and expertise becomes essentially a shortcut.

My geology book has no shortage of terms that I could put onto flashcards. "Monocline," "stratification," "glacial scour"—whip out the Sharpie now. But I could also map out the process of glaciation in a flowchart or some other visual medium. I could make a timeline of the ages of the earth and link it with the most significant geological changes that took place during each era. I can also take down questions that come up that the book either left unanswered or made me want to investigate more fully.

You can use most elements of the book review phase for study planning in the same way. In our European cinema example, you could make a catalog or database for European film directors that outlines their work, their main themes, or their stylistic choices. You can draw up flashcards that will help you recall the important facets of different European strains: "neo-realism," "giallo horror," "spaghetti Western," and "cinéma du look." And of course you can journal what you've learned, either in written form or some visual expression.

The SQ3R method is no joke. It's exhaustive and detailed and will take patience and sharp organization to pull off. But if you give yourself the patience and devotion to take each step seriously and slowly, you'll find it incredibly helpful to tackle a complex subject. And each time you do it, it's a little easier than the last.

Takeaways

- Previewing a text essentially involves gathering all the relevant information that you need to know about a text before reading it. This can involve basic details such as the title of the text, its synopsis, index, etc., or you could use more elaborate methods of previewing to familiarize yourself more intimately with the text.
- One more complex method is the KBG method. Here, you first note all the basic details such as the title, headings, etc. Then, you proceed to the introduction, conclusion, the first line after every heading, and things like learning objectives. Finally, you note down what you already know about the main theme that the text is based on, what biases you have about the text or its ideas/themes, and the learning goals you have in mind for the text.

- Another similar method is the 4 Ps method, the four Ps being purpose, previewing, prior knowledge, and prediction. Like the KBG method, note why you're reading the text, then go over the rudimentary parts of the book such as its title and headings. Following this, think about what you already know about the text's main themes, and finally, make some educated predictions about what the author is going to say about these themes.
- The last previewing method is called the THIEVES method. Here, you go over the title, headings, introduction, first sentence after every heading, the visual aids, the questions at the end of each chapter, and the summaries if there are any.

Chapter 3. Speed-Reading Meat and Bones

Reading—you've done it since you were a child. What do you have to learn about it? It turns out, you probably have never learned how to read quickly and efficiently. Whatever you've been doing has been adequate to get by, but learning to read better and retain more information is a skill in itself. It's not just the passive absorption of information that you've grown accustomed to.

Chances are, whatever you learn and study, you will eventually have to read about it. The more you read, the better, which means the faster and more efficiently you read, the faster and more efficient your learning will be. How do we reach that point?

You can often make yourself an expert on an intellectual subject just by reading enough in that area. But despite the incredible importance of reading, most of us are wildly inefficient at it. Like a child that never goes beyond a crawl, most people have enough reading skills to move around, but they are far from running.

The average adult reads at a speed of 300 words per minute. You can take various reading and comprehension tests online to test your current abilities if you'd like to discover your word-per-minute rate. According to a speed-reading test conducted by Staples, here's how many words per minute people read on average:

- Third-grade students: 150 wpm
- Eighth-grade students: 250 wpm
- Average adult: 300 wpm
- Average university student: 450 wpm
- Average business executive: 575 wpm
- Average university professor: 675 wpm

Obviously this is not so good for our self-learning quest. Think about the difference if you could add even 100 words more per minute. You would be able to finish a book 25–33 percent faster. You would be able to spend more time on what matters—analyzing and thinking about the information as opposed to simply absorbing it. Or you would just finish your reading and have more time to spend on your other pursuits and hobbies.

This chapter will be about teaching you how to read faster, as well as retain more. You will get the best of both worlds. It's important to note that speed reading as a concept of reading a book in minutes is largely a myth. A few special savants and geniuses in the world may be able to do it, but for the rest of us, our mere mortal brains can't process things like a computer.

In this chapter, we'll cover four of the top tips in training yourself to read faster while retaining more information at the same time—for mortals. You'll see for yourself (eventually, not immediately!) that speed reading itself is not a myth, and you can use it in your quest for better learning. What's ahead are the following: how to stop subvocalizing, training your eyes to widen and spread, how to strategically skim for important information, and how to maintain better focus and attention. We'll start with subvocalizations.

Stop Subvocalizations

What are subvocalizations?

When you started to read, you probably read out loud. Your elementary-school teacher wanted you to read the book and say the words aloud. After you mastered this skill, you were told to simply say the words inside your head and read quietly. As we also noted earlier, the parts of our brain that control language comprehension also control speech, which points toward a fundamental biological link between reading words and saying them. This is further evidenced by the fact that a person's average reading speed is often the same as their talking speed.

When it comes to reading, we are often limited by the time that it takes for our subconscious mind to pronounce the words on the page. We don't say them out loud, but our mind speaks them unconsciously: this is known as "subvocalizing." This is where most reading education and skill levels end.

To move to a new level, you need to stop sounding the words inside your head. Subvocalizing takes time—more time than is necessary to comprehend the words you are reading. It is almost impossible to go much beyond 400 or 500 words per minute while subvocalizing. And even then, it sounds like you are having a heart attack because you are speaking so fast inside your mind.

When we speak a word out loud, it takes a certain amount of time to pronounce. However, we do not actually need to pronounce words when we read. We can simply absorb them. To do this, you need to train yourself to read without hearing the words in your head.

If someone reads at around a thousand words per minute (entirely possible and trainable), there is no way they could hear the words in their heads while trying to process them. Instead, they simply see the word and their brains extract the meaning of what was written. It's about processing the meaning without speaking the words out loud—this is the essence of stopping subvocalizations, and it doesn't sound easy because it's a tough habit to break!

Since most people currently can't separate subvocalization from comprehension, they are locked in at a rate of about 400–500 words per minute. Moving beyond that rate requires you to embrace that ***your mind and eyes read faster than your mouth.***

Start by picking out any word in a paragraph and look at it for a moment in total silence. Look at it, and instead of repeating the word mentally, think about what it represents and means. Think about its meaning. You can even just describe it mentally instead of reading it out loud inside your head. There will still be a slight bit of subvocalization, but by merely observing words without the desire to pronounce them, the new habit will begin to form on its own.

This part might feel obscure or abstract in the beginning, and that's totally normal. It might even feel impossible, and that's natural too because you are fundamentally changing how you take in information. All you need to be concerned with is looking at words without the desire to hear the way they sound.

Next, pick a sentence somewhere or even write it yourself. Now, instead of subvocalizing when you read it, try a few things to see if they work for you.

First, picture it visually in your mind. Second, hum to yourself as you read it, so you literally can't read it because of the humming. Third, in the same vein, you can practice reading while chewing gum on the same premise that it makes it difficult to subconsciously subvocalize. The logic behind humming and chewing gum is that these work as effective distractions, just like playing music in the background while you read. Music is a particularly potent option because not only does it help stop the subvocalizations, but it also improves overall concentration while reading.

However, keep in mind that not all types of music will achieve this goal. Something like heavy metal or anything with a strong beat will likely distract you too much, and lower your overall reading speed. Choose something soft, like classical music, or anything that is more instrumental than lyrical.

A fourth step you might want to use while trying to stop subvocalizations is a visual pacer. This can be a pen, pencil, or even your finger, anything that helps you keep track of words on a page. This improves focus, reduces subvocalization, and also helps you do something called word-chunking. More on that later.

Another novel way in which you can use the same principle is to occupy the subvocalizing voice in your head with another voice. The next time you read, try counting in your head simultaneously. As you do this, fixate your eyes first at the start of the sentence, then at the middle, and finally toward the end. You are occupying your inner voice with something else but allowing the processing to occur. Practice as much as you can, and eventually you won't feel the need to subvocalize to understand words.

For instance, take a sentence like "The bees are coming." Visualize what that looks like instead of saying the words themselves. That's where you start.

Subvocalizations can be tough to eliminate, but it's pretty clear that you can think faster than you can talk, so you can see how important this is to reading faster. When you're reading something incredibly complex with a lot of jargon and technical terminology, you might be forced to fall back on subvocalization to maintain a fast enough reading speed because tricks like visualization, playing music, etc., might not work. Also, when you're reading for pleasure, there isn't anything to be gained from reading as fast as you can, but you probably won't enjoy the book as much if you do so. In these scenarios, subvocalizations can be a good thing since reading speed isn't the priority. However, by and large, you can afford to minimize subvocalization because the net result will be an increase in reading speed which will allow you to acquire more knowledge.

The next step in reading faster is to train and exercise your eyes—get them into shape for reading faster. Your eyes are muscles too, after all, so you must train them for the bigger workload you are going to give them.

Train Your Eyes

The next major step in learning to read faster and more efficiently is to train your eyes. Your eyes are muscles, so they need to be exercised and prepared for reading faster. Obviously, increasing your reading speed will require a bigger workload on your eyes than you are used to. If you read for leisure, your eyes may barely move, but speed-reading is a focus activity that takes time and effort—with big payoffs.

With so-called normal reading, your eyes don't stay fixed in one spot when reading. Eye-tracking studies have shown that your eyes actually quiver and move around considerably. These are called *saccades*. And every movement away from your position in text requires a few milliseconds to readjust and refocus. All of these minuscule readjustments in locating your place in a book add up to be very costly to your reading speed.

So you're not actually training yourself to move your eyes *more*—rather, you are training them to move *less* and in a more controlled way to not waste energy and effort. It's easier than you think, though it might make you feel like you are back in grade school at first.

There are two ways to do this. The first is to use your finger, or any other object, as a pointer. The second is to strengthen your peripheral vision and learn to focus on chunks of words rather than individual ones.

Using a finger to guide yourself while reading is often considered to be reserved for children and then forgotten once they have the hang of reading. It's important because it keeps you on track and makes sure you aren't distracted or wasting energy.

This trick comes in handy again while learning to speed read. Use your index finger to mark where you are on the page at all times. It should follow along with the word you are currently reading, slowly scrolling across each line and then back down one. It may feel awkward at first and may even temporarily slow your reading rate as you adjust, but using a pointer is critical if you want to improve your reading skill.

By moving your finger more quickly than you can actually read, your eyes get used to viewing text faster than your brain can process what is written down. This will break your subvocalization attachment and can easily let you increase your reading rate with sufficient practice.

When using a pointer, your primary goal is to move the pointer at a very consistent pace. You should not stop your finger or slow it down. It should simply slide from one side of the text to the other at a uniform speed.

Go ahead and try it right now with any writing that is in front of you. You can even pause this lesson for a minute to attempt it. You might feel silly, but you'll find that using a finger will focus your eye movements and even push you to a faster speed.

One of the biggest and easiest epiphanies in your journey to becoming a speed reader will be in recognizing how much your eyes move while you read. For the average person, their eyes cannot keep moving in a single, fluid line without needing to backtrack. If you begin to pay attention to your eyes, I can guarantee that you will start to notice just how often you move back, then forward, then back again. In the long run, this adds entire hours to your reading experience, and it might even prevent you from finishing in the first place.

The second part of exercising your eyes, besides using a pointer and calming your excess eye movements, is to deal with *eye fixation*. An eye fixation is a location on the page where your eye comes to a stop. Readers who make fewer eye fixations read faster because they take in more words with each fixation.

The wider your vision span, the more words you can process in an eye fixation and the faster you can read—and, of course, the fewer eye fixations you make on any given page. Here's an example so that you can test this out. Read this sentence: the rain in Spain stays mainly in the plain. For the average reader, they would need a single eye fixation for every word because of the nature of the sentence. But someone with a wider vision span would need only about two or three fixations because they can take in more text at a time. When multiple words in this sentence are absorbed together, they can be processed faster than if you do so individually. So to deal with eye fixation, we must widen how much we can see at one time. Acquiring the ability to see many words at a time is essential for speed reading. The goal is to stop looking at a single word at a time and instead start learning how to look at chunks of words.

Through this process, you are trying to strengthen your peripheral vision. *Macular vision* is your primary focus. When you look directly at something, you see with your macular vision. *Peripheral vision* is what you see less distinctly in the area outside your macular vision. Because receptor cells on the retina of your eye are concentrated at the center and less concentrated toward the edges, colors and shapes are harder to distinguish in peripheral vision (although you can quickly pick up on motion).

But you can see to the left, to the right, above, and below the area bordered by your macular vision. The point is, your peripheral vision needs to improve to read faster and reduce eye fixations, so exercise your eyes to strengthen this ability.

There are six muscles attached to each of your eyes. These muscles control all the movements your eyes make, including those that make your eyes look up, down, and all around. Eye muscles also help your eyes focus on near objects and things that are far away. Just like any other muscle in your body, exercise helps your eye muscles gain strength and flexibility. And just like other muscles, there are specially designed exercises that help build eye muscle strength and flexibility.

Here is a simple eye exercise designed to help build eye muscle flexibility and enhance your reading speed.

To start, sit or stand and focus your vision straight ahead. Next, stretch each hand out to the side like you used to do when pretending you were an airplane. Stick each thumb up toward the sky and hold that pose.

Now, keeping your head straight, move your eyes to the right until you can see your thumb. If you can't quite see it, just stretch your eyes as far to the right side as you can. Then glance to the left while making sure you keep your head still and facing straight ahead. This is one repetition. Try not to move your head, only your eyes, so you are stretching your eyes to each side and working the muscles involved.

Continue glancing right to left and left to right nine more times. That is one set of ten repetitions. Repeat the sequence of ten glances to each side for a total of three sets. Your eyes should feel pretty tired at the end of it; it will be a weird and unfamiliar feeling.

It may not seem like it, but this act of stretching and working your eye muscles will widen your sphere of vision. Where you previously could only focus on one word, you now have the ability to visually focus on two or three. As your peripheral eye muscles get stronger, you might even evolve to seeing an entire line of text in one glance. The point is, even if you only double your focus by seeing two words at a time, you have effectively doubled your reading speed just by training your eyes. This technique, along with using a pointer finger or object, will hugely aid you in better reading.

The next step in reading better is about strategically skimming information and drawing out the important parts by knowing what to look for and what you can skip.

Word-Chunking

In the previous section, we discussed how you can broaden your vision to see more words than the average reader. But being able to see them is only half the story. You also need to process the words together at fast enough rate to increase your overall reading speed. This process is called word-chunking.

The easiest way to learn to read more words at a time is to simply practice. You can do it right away while reading this book. Try to take in three words at a time and continue reading for as long as you can before you feel like you're losing track of what is being said. The process is much easier than it sounds, and you'll likely be surprised by how much quicker you can read as a result. Still, this is a mode of reading that we're not used to, and only practice will change that. Once you can take in three words at a time comfortably, you can start practicing with four words, and then maybe even five. This is where the skills you learned in the previous section will come in handy, since you've trained your eyes to be able to take in more words at a time.

An excellent resource to help you with this is [Ron Cole's Alchemy Educational Training website](https://superreading.com/eyehop/) (https://superreading.com/eyehop/). This website contains several custom pdfs for two, three, four, and five-word chunks (or "hops" as Cole calls them) so that you can practice taking in those quantities of words at a time. You can also create your own such pdf through the website. If there's an article or chunk of text you want to practice word chunking, you can simply enter it into the website and choose how many words you want chunked together. So, if you choose three, there'll be a slightly bigger space after every third word to make it easier for you to take in particular sets of words at a time.

You might wonder whether not reading words individually will lead to missing out on important concepts or ideas and merely understanding the gist of what is being said in a text. This fear is unfounded and likely influenced by the insistence of our teachers in childhood to read each word for better understanding. It served a purpose then, but we don't need to do the same thing now. Individual words cannot carry concepts or ideas; these are only expressed in groups of words. If you can learn to read these groups of words at a fast rate while maintaining comprehension, you won't miss out on anything important. In fact, you're likely to absorb more information quicker instead of leaving things halfway through because it takes too long to read.

Strategically Skim

The next step in reading faster is to understand how to strategically skim your material—after stopping subvocalizations and training your eyes. For most of us, skimming has a negative connotation. It's when we are rushed for time and can only look at the first sentence of each paragraph—or whatever method you decide makes sense. What we're discussing here is a different type of skimming entirely.

Frankly, not all information is created equally, and this can be true even within sentences and paragraphs. There are some things that are destined to waste our time in reading, so we should learn exactly what is okay to skip, what to focus on, and how to manage all of that. Skimming information in our context is about saving time and being able to see through what's in front of you.

Here, we are skimming in a way that lets you retain just as much, just by cutting the fat. Traditional skimming would be skipping about 75 percent of the content—here, we are only skipping 25 percent. How are we accomplishing this? There are three interrelated methods we can use.

First, start and stop reading three words from the margin of the pages.

By default, we always start reading the first word on the left of the page and go all the way to the last word on the right. We've been taught to be thorough and leave no stone unturned. But here's the trick: you can start on the third word from the left and stop three words from the end, and your peripheral vision just might pick up the first two and last two words automatically.

In a line of ten words, this allows you to "read" only six words and save 40 percent of the effort and time. This obviously adds up quite quickly. As with all these techniques, stop the course and try it for a second. Does it feel odd? Does it feel like you are skipping important information? Just try it out and you'll find that you aren't missing anything necessary for comprehension—your brain will fill it in, and you'll be able to figure it out through the context of the sentence.

Second, skip *meaningless* words.

To be clear, skipping small words isn't quite the same thing as skimming what you're reading. When you skim, you're not retaining the words or ideas that you're consuming. You may have a general sense of the work, but the fine details will likely be lost.

Learning how to read faster is all about eliminating the small, unnecessary words that fill up a page. Not every word is created equal. There are plenty of obscure little words that don't help you, and forcing yourself to read them can only hurt your efforts. These words certainly have their place, of course, and we need them to construct sentences and ideas! But when we're trying to read quickly, we can often skip these words with no ill-effects: "if," "is," "to," "the," "and," "was."

The best part of skipping the small words is that they do not contribute anything useful, so bypassing them effectively means that you are getting more out of your reading experience in less time. If you are reading a fiction or poetry book and you want to appreciate the prose and sentence structure, this tip may not work for you. But then again, you wouldn't be trying to read those books quickly anyway!

Let's look at an example sentence that uses some of those useless words. "**The** dog went inside **the** house, **and** ate his dinner, which **was** leftover spaghetti." How many words can you eliminate from that sentence? At least four or five. The sentence is 14 words. That's one-third of the sentence!

A useful method that can help you skip unnecessary words is called the zig-zag method. This is similar to using a pacer at a constant speed and in a linear direction, but with one crucial difference. Instead of going from left to right, you go in a zig-zag direction. Try reading the same sentence above, but take your finger up and down instead of from left to right and read only the words where your finger lands. You'll notice that you still ended up reading the gist of the sentence even though you read significantly fewer words than what the sentence contains. As you read, you'll notice that filler words are generally conjunctions or prepositions, and the important bits of the sentences are usually nouns and verbs. Keep this in mind as you read and practice and you'll learn to spot them quicker as you go.

Third, scan for *important* words. This is related to the previous point of ignoring useless words. When you can identify what matters in a sentence, that understanding is all that is needed. As you read any given sentence, you will probably get 90 percent of the meaning from 50 percent of the words, and for the purposes of learning at a quick pace, the rest of the words are unnecessary filler.

For example, "I went to the vet yesterday because my cat was sick." That is an 11-word sentence.

What are the important words in that sentence? "Vet," "yesterday," "cat," and "sick." These are only four words we've pulled from the sentence, and everything else isn't necessary to get the meaning. You can absolutely get the meaning of the sentence just from those words. This is easier to do than the previous step and also allows you to save more time from the so-called meaningless and useless words.

Let's have another easy example. "I want to go to China because I hear the food is very tasty and the people are nice."

How many words do you really need to get the meaning in that sentence? "Want," "go," "China," "food," "tasty," "people," and "nice." That's seven words out of 19 for the sentence. You can see how valuable this method can be.

Scanning paragraphs like this takes practice, but it can greatly increase your reading speed. And the beauty is that if you scan through a paragraph and don't completely grasp the meaning, you just go back, slow down, and add the words back in until it makes sense. Then take off again.

Strategically skimming information is probably not what you initially thought it was. Most people think of skimming as quickly going through information and missing all the vital parts. But here, skimming involves learning how to parse information and only read what is needed to get the meaning and understanding. It's tougher but very rewarding in your path to learning better and reading faster.

Miscellaneous Strategies to Read Faster

Above, we discussed some major improvements you can make to the way you read in order to increase your reading speed, and we also went over some tricks to help you do so. In this section, we'll discuss some more tricks that you can employ to read faster.

Once you've experimented and practiced the above tricks a few times, you can move on to timing yourself as you read. To do this, set the timer on one minute and choose a text you can practice speed reading on. Start the timer and read normally, going over as much of the text as you can. Once the timer runs down, make a note of how far you got.

Now, use every single speed-reading strategy in your arsenal and read the same text again over one minute and see how far you go. Chances are that you ended up going over more of the text than when you tried reading normally. This is a great way of tricking your mind into challenging yourself by setting benchmarks for you to beat the next time you attempt this technique. Take note of how many words you covered in the one minute you read using speed-reading techniques.

The next time you time yourself, try to beat your previous score of words read. Pushing yourself to read faster is one of the best ways to ensure that you do, and timing yourself challenges you in a healthy manner that results in improvements.

The next tip comes from Abby Marks Beale, America's number-one speed-reading expert, and it's one that will reduce your reading time many times over. According to Beale, writers tend to follow a common method when conveying any sort of information. They start each paragraph with a sentence that introduces its purpose and gives you a fair idea of what's going to be discussed in it. They also end paragraphs with a reaffirmation of the idea that was expressed in the first line through a brief summarization. As such, she recommends that you can often get away with reading just the first and last line of paragraphs and understand most of what is being said.

This is especially true of scientific and academic journals, since they contain a lot of technical information that a layperson wouldn't understand anyway. The next time you're reading something complex, try this method and compare it to reading a portion of the text word by word. Notice how much information you missed while reading only the first and last lines of each paragraph. Chances are you wouldn't have missed much.

This last tip is not a strategy as such, but a general tip to follow that will improve your overall reading speed, and that is to improve your vocabulary. To some extent this will naturally occur if you read more, but you can speed up the process by reading non-fiction or more scholarly work since writers in academia tend to write in more formal language.

Expanding your vocabulary improves reading speed because, when you're reading and come across a word that you don't know the meaning of, you end up wasting time trying to figure out the context in which it is used. This brings back a lot of rudimentary reading tendencies such as going back to re-read words, and the result is that you end up reading slower. However, if you already know what the word means, you skip this issue altogether.

Takeaways

- This chapter has a dual focus. It emphasizes speed reading as well as retaining the most content that you can through primarily three techniques.
- First, we need to eliminate subvocalizations. This is the practice of saying words in your head as you repeat them. Subvocalizations significantly reduce the speed at which we can read. However, getting rid of this tendency will take time since this practice has been ingrained in most of us. To practice reading without subvocalizations, try to distract yourself with soft music in the background while reading. Use visual

pacers like a finger to read, and chewing gum also helps you to subvocalize less.
- Next, we need to train our eyes read better. Most of us are unaware of how much our eyes move back and forth while reading. This slows us down because we end up re-reading words we've already read. We need to train our eyes to stay fixed, and we also need to enable our eyes to take in more words at a time. We tend to focus on each word individually, but with practice, we can read two to five words simultaneously.
- The third strategy here is to skim effectively and smartly. We do this by skipping three words from the margin on every line, both on the left and right since these are picked up by our peripheral vision anyway. We also need to skip meaningless words while reading because they do not improve our understanding of the main ideas and concepts in the book. Lastly, we need to scan the text for important words. These are usually nouns or verbs, whereas conjunctions and prepositions can generally be bypassed.

Chapter 4. Improving Comprehension and Retention

Speed reading is often associated with a loss in comprehension and retention. The faster you read, the less of it can be fully processed and thus retained, or so goes the claim. While there is some truth to this, the consequences of speed reading on comprehension and retention have been highly exaggerated. Moreover, there are things you can do to comprehend and retain as much as possible while also gradually increasing your reading speed.

It is true that beyond a point, reading too fast will inevitably result in loss of comprehension. However, whether this a good or bad thing ultimately depends on what you're reading. If you're reading a Dan Brown novel, some loss of comprehension won't do much damage. The same applies to newspaper articles and other mundane forms of media. However, increasing your reading speed to a point where comprehension becomes endangered is in itself a challenge and will take much time and practice.

Remember, the average adult can read up to 300 words per minute. You can go up to 500 words per minute without losing any comprehension or retention whatsoever. If you were to just increase your reading speed by 200 words per minute, that in itself would be a huge improvement. The current speed-reading champion can read about 4700 words per minute with a 62 percent comprehension rate. So, even if you were to go slightly above the 500 words per minute mark, you would only marginally reduce your comprehension or retention.

All of this is to say that while concerns about understanding and retaining information are valid, you are likely a long way off from having to worry about them. Speed reading isn't just about mindlessly reading as fast as you can. That's a trap which *will* ensure you comprehend and retain less. Instead, if you prioritize comprehension and retention from the start and apply speed-reading strategies like the ones discussed above while keeping that in mind, it is very much possible to read fast and understand everything simultaneously.

In the previous chapters, we've discussed several tips and tricks that are aimed at doing just this by scrapping the filler and focusing on the crux of the content in your text. This chapter goes over more such tips and strategies with a specific focus on comprehending and retaining as much content as possible. First, we'll start out with same basic, elementary things you can do to keep your retention levels high. Then, we'll jump into specific strategies relating to visualization, eye fitness, reading for ideas, etc.

Basic Tips to Improve Comprehension and Retention

As promised, we'll first go over some very basic elements that contribute to your overall reading speed, retention, and comprehension. These can be fixed either immediately or over time with some conscious attention, but there aren't specific "strategies" you need to use for them. Some of these might even go without saying, but it's nice to be aware of them so that you can squeeze every bit of productivity out of your reading time.

The first set of things you can do relate to your environment. Making these small changes to the physical location where you read can make a world of difference to how much you end up retaining from your text. The first thing to do is avoid major distractions. As we discussed earlier, some light distraction in the form of soft music can help you stop subvocalizations and thus read faster. But if the space you read in is frequently filled with loud noises, your comprehension and retention levels go down. Similarly, ensure there are no electronic gadgets that might take your attention away from reading.

Next, you'll want to keep your room tidy and clean. Make your desk neat and ensure your bed isn't too cluttered. Ensure your room is well lit and the temperature isn't too hot or cold. If you can have natural light through a big open window, that's better than having artificial lights on. Also, if you can have plants in your reading space, they will have a calming influence which will ultimately improve your comprehension and retention levels by improving focus. Lastly, avoid reading on your bed, because this can cause feelings of lethargy and impact your overall sleep quality.

Now that we've gotten the environmental factors out of the way, we'll discuss a second and arguably more important set of things you can do to improve your reading comprehension and retention. Primary among these is becoming more well-read. This subsumes many other smaller benefits you reap as a result that can also be focused upon individually. These include improving your vocabulary, your language fluency, and recognition of various types of phrases like the ones we outlined above.

Above all, reading well also helps you gain knowledge from various disciplines and on many different topics which will impact the way you think about and preview the texts you read. When you engage with arguments and themes in books like *Freakonomics* after having read other books on economics, the end learning outcomes are much richer and more productive than if you went in without knowing much about economics at all. Moreover, your pre-existing familiarity with certain topics allows you to connect your newly acquired knowledge to things you already knew, and this is one of the best ways to comprehend and retain more.

In addition to this, being well read gives you the advantage of being able to process words and sentences faster. Not only does it give you much-needed practice, but it also familiarizes you with words and phrases that you otherwise might not have known about. This prevents you from having to refer to a dictionary repeatedly, allowing you instead to simply move on with the text.

Now, you might be wondering how exactly you can become well read, and the truth is there is no one way to do so. The best way is to just pick up books and articles on as broad a set of topics and disciplines as you can find. To make the process easier, you can make a list of all the topics you want to cover and compile some books related to them. Choose short books so that you can do this in a reasonable amount of time and keep ticking each one off as you complete your target. Eventually, you'll notice all the benefits that come from being well read and how it impacts the books you read next.

Visualization

Now that we've gone over some basic things you can do to improve your comprehension and retention in the long-term, it's time to discuss some concrete strategies you can implement to achieve the same goal sooner. The first one we'll discuss is among the most powerful tricks you can add to your arsenal while speed reading, and this is visualization.

Visualization is such a powerful tool for speed reading because humans are largely visual creatures. We've relied on sight for survival throughout history. Even today, visual information forms over 70 percent of our daily sensory input. However, language isn't a natural skill that humans always possessed. It has been learned and ingrained over centuries of evolution. Thus, when we read words, we need to be able to translate them into pictures for maximum comprehension.

This activity is called dynamic comprehension, wherein you form a series of images in your head as you read in order to understand what's written instead of subvocalizing or repeating words in your head. As we've discussed, it's difficult to stop subvocalizing but if you manage to replace that with visualization, you'll become a skilled reader with great comprehension and retention.

A good way to start testing and practicing this skill is to begin with reading fictional books. It's much easier to visualize a story because you can get inside the visual field of each character if the author's descriptive skills are good. It's hard to immediately start visualizing material from complex text, and reading fiction will help you gradually build your skills so that you can eventually learn to speed read through visualization with difficult material. Once you're comfortable with stories that easily lend themselves to visualization, you can move on to more technical texts.

As you use fictional texts to practice visualization, there are some tips you should keep in mind. First, be regular and try to practice visualization every day, even if it is for short periods of time. Second, be as detailed in your visualizations as you can possibly be. Fantasy fiction is particularly useful for this because of the world-building in it, so the *Game of Thrones* books or those by Brandon Sanderson may be worth a try. Be sure to take breaks, as extensive visualization can be tiring when you first start out.

Besides reading, there are types of visualization exercises you can engage in which will help you while you read. These are fairly basic and won't consume much time, but are excellent ways to practice this skill. For starters, you can take any picture you have on your phone and look at it carefully for as long as you need. Then, close your eyes and recount every detail in as excruciating detail as you can. Once you feel you've recounted as much as you remember, look at the picture again and see how you fared.

Try it again with a different picture after a few minutes. You can repeat this same exercise with objects, places and people as well, with the minor difference that you must rotate them in your mind so that you recount every miniscule detail. Keep practicing till you feel yourself becoming more and more comfortable with visualization. Eventually, the activity will become less energy-consuming and you'll also notice the difference it makes to your reading speed.

Ocular Fitness

After visualization, another invaluable tool for improving your comprehension and retention is your eye fitness. This essentially involves widening your vision span so that you can see more words at a time. Normally, your eyes move and settle on each individual word before going to the next one. This is an extremely inefficient process which takes up too much time that can be cut down. Once you widen your vision span, you'll be able to read more words at a time, which means that your eyes don't need to waste time by fixating on each individual word. Instead you can process chunks of them simultaneously, and increase your overall reading speed.

The chief actor in this drama is your peripheral vision. Your peripheral vision determines all the things you can see outside your main area of focus. So, if you're looking straight ahead, you can probably still see some things at the edges of your vision span, though not clearly. Regardless, those objects are registered by your eyes and processed in your brain because you are, in fact, seeing them. Though in real life this is only useful in dangerous situations, peripheral vision can become an extremely handy tool while reading because you don't necessarily have to read words properly for them to be registered and understood by your brain.

The problem is, because peripheral vision is so rarely used in our daily life, its highly likely that your vision span isn't very long. As such, it needs to be trained and lengthened in order for it to be useful while reading. There is only one major way to train your eyes to see more at the peripheries, and that is by exercising them. There are several different exercises you can cycle between so that things don't become monotonous. If you're regular and persistent, you'll experience results soon enough.

Before we dive into the major techniques, there are some minor things you can also do to improve your overall eyesight. This will contribute to your peripheral vision and improve your reading speed too. One of the most important things you can to do improve your eyesight overall is to eat a healthy diet. There are a variety of foods that are good for your eyes, such as carrots, eggs, lean meats, salmon, sweet potatoes, etc. Incorporate these into your meals.

Avoid smoking. Eye infections are one in the long list of diseases you'll avoid by giving up this habit. Smoking also makes it four times more likely that you will develop age-related macular degeneration and cataracts, which is a major cause of blindness across the world.

Avoid squinting as much as possible because doing so narrows your field of vision. Relax your eyes at regular intervals when using screens, especially if you're doing so for extended periods of time. Blink regularly because it relaxes the muscles around your eyes and stops you from squinting as well. Lastly, avoid the use of sunglasses. They prevent lights of certain wavelengths from entering your eyes, and this impacts their overall health. They may also cause radiation to build up in your eyes, which can be disastrous for you in the long run.

With the minor measures out of the way, we can now get to the part where we discuss exercises. A few have been covered before, and some more will be listed here.

The 20-20-20 Exercise

The first exercise is called 20-20-20. Here, what you need to do is alternate between viewing something that is close to you, like a screen, and something that is at least 20 or more feet away. This avoids strain on your eyes and exercises them efficiently. It's called the 20-20-20 exercise because you must do it every 20 minutes, for 20 seconds, by looking at something 20 feet or more away.

Eye Writing

Another handy exercise is called eye writing. Look at a blank wall around you and move your eyeballs in a manner that resembles how you would move a pen or pencil while writing alphabets. You can simply run through alphabets from A to Z or use specific words to make things slightly more interesting. Ensure that you do not move your head at all while doing this exercise so that your eyes are doing all the work. With practice, this will strengthen your ocular muscles and improve their flexibility as well as their range of motion.

Clock Gazing

A third excellent exercise for eyes is called clock gazing. For this, you need to sit somewhere with an erect spine and imagine a giant analogue clock in front of you. Now, look from the twelve o'clock position to the six o'clock position. Next, take your eyes from the center to the one o'clock position, and then to seven o'clock. After that, from two o'clock to eight o'clock, and so on until you reach twelve and six o'clock again.

After all of these exercises, ensure that you gently palm your eyes. This just involves rubbing your palms together for a few seconds to generate warmth and then placing them in front of your eyes. Then, gently massage the bony areas around your eyes with the outside of your palm for 30 seconds. Lastly, cover your eyes and gaze into total darkness for a few moments before resuming other activities.

Reading for Ideas

The best way to get better at speed reading while retaining and comprehending the most you can is by learning from those who have mastered the skill. There are several phony speed-reading experts online who continue peddling their wares, but there are also some real gems which can help you learn a lot about the process and the activity. Of these, we're going to discuss one particular book that can be the most useful to you in your speed-reading journey. This book is called *Speed Reading with Your Right Brain: Learn to Read Ideas Instead of Just Words* by David Butler.

We've chosen this book because it captures the central theme that we've been trying to expound in this chapter. That theme is that speed reading, or reading super fast, is useless unless you comprehend the information you're reading as well. This is why we've focused on maintaining comprehension and retention while also improving reading speeds, and Butler attempts to do the same through his book.

Butler's work also captures the emphasis on visualization that we've been focusing on throughout, along with the idea that individual words do not convey much. It is only when they're grouped together that you see ideas and concepts forming. This shows that you need not go through each word individually like you were taught to as a child; you can easily take in multiple words at the same time and still comprehend things as efficiently as you did in your former reading method.

This is exactly why Butler focuses on the right brain so much—it's the part of the brain which is responsible for visualization. He believes that the key to speed reading, or as he calls it, "speed-comprehension," lies not in relying on your left hemisphere, which is generally responsible for language comprehension and speech, but your right hemisphere, which handles visualization.

The book has its own methods and frameworks for encouraging readers to visualize their way through learning and reading, and it will undoubtedly be an enriching experience to read this book and that one in conjunction. You could also use many of the tricks you've learnt in this book while reading Butler's and compare which methods and strategies suit you best.

Retention

So far in this chapter, we've been focusing on comprehension and retention together. However, for this section, we're going to concentrate exclusively on the latter because, after all, they're two related but separate things. By improving your retention, you ensure that material you consume stays with you longer, and this is ultimately the goal of reading: to acquire knowledge and keep it with you for as long as possible. To that end, we'll discuss several tips and strategies that you can follow which ensure that you retain the most material possible from everything you read.

Take Notes

The first strategy we're going to discuss is not actually a single suggestion but a cluster of them, and they revolve around expressing your thoughts while reading a text. Always ensure that you take notes while reading a text and pen down any thoughts you might have on the subject. You can use the margins, a separate notepad, or individual pages, whichever you prefer.

Underline everything you deem important and copy passages if need be. This process ensures that you're actually engaging with the material you're reading instead of just passively consuming it, making it more likely that you'll remember it in the future.

The German thinker Karl Marx took this method very seriously. While reading complex texts, he would use one page of notes for every page he read of other philosophers. While you need not go that far, the anecdote illustrates the importance and value of engaging with texts on an intellectual level in order to retain and understand things better.

Summarize

The next strategy we'll discuss is closely related to the first one, and this is summarizing each chapter, or even each section that you read in a text. Break down the main ideas that have been expressed in as simple a manner as possible. Alternatively, you could simply note down your main takeaways from that section or chapter in bullet points. This is another way of engaging with the text that gives your memory solid cues about what it should retain by refining a mass of text into much shorter, digestible bites.

Pass on Your Knowledge

Our third strategy will need you to involve a friend, parent, or anyone else willing to listen to you because here, you'll be teaching someone else the things you just learned. This is easily one of the best ways to retain material because it tests how well you've understood the concept, and whether you can break it down in a manner that can be understood by someone else. This makes the technique radically different from the other two we discussed because in those we can often get away with not fully understanding something. But here, we can't. If you succeed in explaining something to another person well, that is a great sign that you yourself have mastered the content. If not, you might want to go over it again.

Use Mind Maps

Our fourth strategy here will be the use of mind maps. These are incredibly simple, yet powerful tools to aggregate everything you've learned in a manner that can be processed visually. They can also be useful for problem solving and finding the missing link in a chain or cluster of related concepts.

To make a mind map, start with a concept in the center. This can be the name of the book, a certain concept, a theme, basically anything that forms the core of everything you've learned. Then, draw branches extending from this main theme toward all directions. At the end of these branches, note down one element that is related to the central theme. So, if you placed economics in the center, one of the branches may contain "law of supply and demand." Another may have "Veblen goods," and so on and so forth.

McDowell's Grid

The fifth strategy to improve your retention is known as "McDowell's Grid." Simply put, this grid is meant to capture your reaction to certain ideas or concepts that you encounter in a text. The idea is that your personal reactions predict, above all else, how likely you are to retain a certain concept, and the grid can be used to examine your reactions to various themes.

Making this grid is simple. You can use a pen and paper or a word processor. All you need is a table with two columns and as many rows as necessary. On the left side, note down any and all ideas or concepts that you encountered in the text. On the right, note your reaction to the concept. Did it fascinate you? Was it boring? Did it make you laugh? Write all of it down. Not only does this grid act as an important summary, but it also lets you see things you're interested in and read more about them in the future.

The Knowledge Tree

Our sixth and last idea is similar to the mind map, but instead of connecting concepts you find within the same text, we'll use this to combine ideas *across* different texts. We'll call this a knowledge tree. Imagine a text as a tree, with some fundamental concepts that make up the trunk, and other smaller ones which reside in the branches. The idea is to link branches from different texts together to boost your learning and improve retention. Since you're connecting new knowledge to things you already knew, your brain is more likely to retain this information.

Takeaways

- Speed reading isn't just about reading as fast as possible. You also need to focus on comprehension and retention, because otherwise reading a lot isn't going to help much.
- Humans are largely visual creatures, making visualization one of the most powerful tools you can use to comprehend and retain more. Practice your visualization skills by reading

fictional stories that lend themselves to visualization easier. You can also practice this skill by using photos, objects, or people and taking a few seconds to observe them closely. Then, close your eyes and recount as many details as you can. As your visualization improves, you'll comprehend better and retain more while speed reading.
- Another necessity of comprehending and retaining more is training your eyes to see more words together. You can do this by training your peripheral vision through a variety of exercises. You can also make smart lifestyle choices such as improving your diet, quitting smoking, and avoiding squinting to keep your eyes healthy for a long time.
- Another great book that echoes many of the ideas expressed in this one is David Butler's *Speed Reading with the Right Brain*. Butler emphasizes the right brain because it is responsible for your visualization, while language comprehension and speech is usually controlled by your left hemisphere. However, we need to gradually move

over and use our right hemisphere more if we are to read quicker while also retaining and comprehending.
- To retain more of what you read, make extensive notes and engage with the text as much as you can. Make summaries of each chapter and write down your thoughts or key takeaways.

Summary Guide

CHAPTER 1. YES, IT'S REAL.

- Reading in the way we normally do can take far too long. In the present day and age, we often don't have the time to sit through hundreds of pages of books. To solve this issue, we must learn how to read faster so that we can get on with our lives. That's what speed reading is all about.
- Speed reading primarily involves two areas of your brain, the Broca's area and Wernicke's area. While the former is involved in language production, the latter controls language comprehension. As we'll see later, these areas are very important when it comes to reducing subvocalizations, which will involve skipping the function of the Broca's area and relying solely on the Wernicke's area.

- Several myths about speed reading abound on the internet. The biggest of these is that speed reading is a myth and does not help you read faster. This is decidedly false. Another common myth is that one can train themselves to read tens of thousands of words per minute, which is not humanly possible. A third myth is that subvocalizations are essential to understanding words properly. While this may be true in some cases, it is certainly not accurate in all of them.
- There are many benefits of speed reading that you can come to experience as you practice the techniques in this book. These include improvements in logic since you engage with texts better, gains in memory and focus because you can only read faster when you concentrate on your text fully, and higher confidence from all the knowledge you'll have acquired in a short period of time.

CHAPTER 2. PRE-READING IS THE WAY

- Previewing a text essentially involves gathering all the relevant information that you need to know about a text before reading it. This can involve basic details such as the title of the text, its synopsis, index, etc., or you could use more elaborate methods of previewing to familiarize yourself more intimately with the text.
- One more complex method is the KBG method. Here, you first note all the basic details such as the title, headings, etc. Then, you proceed to the introduction, conclusion, the first line after every heading, and things like learning objectives. Finally, you note down what you already know about the main theme that the text is based on, what biases you have about the text or its ideas/themes, and the learning goals you have in mind for the text.
- Another similar method is the 4 Ps method, the four Ps being purpose, previewing, prior knowledge, and prediction. Like the KBG method, note why you're reading the text, then go over the rudimentary parts of the book

such as its title and headings. Following this, think about what you already know about the text's main themes, and finally, make some educated predictions about what the author is going to say about these themes.
- The last previewing method is called the THIEVES method. Here, you go over the title, headings, introduction, first sentence after every heading, the visual aids, the questions at the end of each chapter, and the summaries if there are any.

CHAPTER 3. SPEED-READING MEAT AND BONES

- This chapter has a dual focus. It emphasizes speed reading as well as retaining the most content that you can through primarily three techniques.
- First, we need to eliminate subvocalizations. This is the practice of saying words in your head as you repeat them. Subvocalizations significantly reduce the speed at which we can read. However, getting rid of this tendency

will take time since this practice has been ingrained in most of us. To practice reading without subvocalizations, try to distract yourself with soft music in the background while reading. Use visual pacers like a finger to read, and chewing gum also helps you to subvocalize less.
- Next, we need to train our eyes read better. Most of us are unaware of how much our eyes move back and forth while reading. This slows us down because we end up re-reading words we've already read. We need to train our eyes to stay fixed, and we also need to enable our eyes to take in more words at a time. We tend to focus on each word individually, but with practice, we can read two to five words simultaneously.
- The third strategy here is to skim effectively and smartly. We do this by skipping three words from the margin on every line, both on the left and right since these are picked up by our peripheral vision anyway. We also need to skip meaningless words while reading because they do not improve our understanding of the main ideas and

concepts in the book. Lastly, we need to scan the text for important words. These are usually nouns or verbs, whereas conjunctions and prepositions can generally be bypassed.

CHAPTER 4. IMPROVING COMPREHENSION AND RETENTION

- Speed reading isn't just about reading as fast as possible. You also need to focus on comprehension and retention, because otherwise reading a lot isn't going to help much.
- Humans are largely visual creatures, making visualization one of the most powerful tools you can use to comprehend and retain more. Practice your visualization skills by reading fictional stories that lend themselves to visualization easier. You can also practice this skill by using photos, objects, or people and taking a few seconds to observe them closely. Then, close your eyes and recount as many details as you can. As your visualization

improves, you'll comprehend better and retain more while speed reading.
- Another necessity of comprehending and retaining more is training your eyes to see more words together. You can do this by training your peripheral vision through a variety of exercises. You can also make smart lifestyle choices such as improving your diet, quitting smoking, and avoiding squinting to keep your eyes healthy for a long time.
- Another great book that echoes many of the ideas expressed in this one is David Butler's *Speed Reading with the Right Brain*. Butler emphasizes the right brain because it is responsible for your visualization, while language comprehension and speech is usually controlled by your left hemisphere. However, we need to gradually move over and use our right hemisphere more if we are to read quicker while also retaining and comprehending.
- To retain more of what you read, make extensive notes and engage with the text as much as you can. Make summaries of

each chapter and write down your thoughts or key takeaways.

www.ingramcontent.com/pod-product-compliance
Lightning Source LLC
Chambersburg PA
CBHW071352080526
44587CB00017B/3068